Private View

Private View

Jean McCurdy

Four Brown Hens

First published in 2018 by Four Brown Hens
30 Victoria Road, Oxford, OX2 7QD, UK

Poems copyright © The Estate of the late Jean McCurdy 2018
Illustrations copyright © Sara Thielker 2018

ISBN: 978-1-9995932-0-9

A CIP record for this book is available from the British Library

Designed and typeset by Holywell Press, holywellpress.com
Printed in Great Britain by Holywell Press, Ltd., Oxford

In memory of Jean

Contents

Knottings

Black Queen

She smirks
under her wrinkled crown.
Among her protégés, surveys
the scene. Her aim – find ways
and means to bring him down,
whose steps she might have followed in.

She watches, and will wait, to twist,
cajole, and stake her claiming wish;
five poisoned darts, speak silky gibberish,
shoot arrows to the lips that kissed
her once. Wait by the exit door,

until he falters. Then she smiles
across the shiny chequered floor,
sidles towards him. Can he afford
another step facing such guile?
He looks for some retreat.

His head high still, his heart is low.
He cannot know her will or whim
covert below smooth rounded skin,
the ebonied veneer of tenderness
that glossed his queen – lost love –
    checkmate!

Adam and Eve

Adam, an old man now,
badgered by data; sick,
from an overdose of printer's ink;
addled by space, speed,
lasers, digits; shuffles
for a last round, keeps
the joker, but has
lost the heart,
(it slipped between his ribs
when Eve departed).

She, freed from her cage,
enticed by mellow scent and taste,
ate, sang and danced, understanding
where the heart had gone,
buried under the dry rubble
of reason. Too much knowing
had gnawed at their
proud bones,
eroding the smile
they should have shared.

Too little wisdom left
important things unsaid, upset
the balance of the garden swing,

tipped Eden upside down.
Eve glancing back, regrets;
takes Adam by the hand,
leads down a path to spaces
where, among the wilderness,
another garden could be laid
afresh, sown wisely,
with a proper reverence
for heart, head, hand and eye,
and that long venerable tree's
sustaining fruit.

Arachne Spins Words

She had a way with words,
could spin them,
like a lightly twisted thread;
could make shapes then,
from edgy situations,
ease us out of awkwardness,
reassure.

I saw her once at work,
throwing the first
important line out into space.
Seeing it make contact, straightaway
she found means to cement
its delicate adherence;
then moved on.

Treading from point to point,
she spun a framework
for our fumbling words, pulled each strand
taut. Made in our midst
a centred anchor, where we felt
secure, attached to one another,
sensing a pattern.

As experts in their craft
are deft with warp
and weft, she executes her plan.
Instinct is her guide.
Establishment complete, she slips away.
Her lacy scaffolding is under way;
she can hide.

The White Queen

She stands
serenely crowned, poised; takes stock.
Sees, consults her entourage,
Bishop, Knight, pawn, help to gauge
what darkening mood
this sovereign's lordly stance reveals.

He, consistent with his dignity,
holds back. In single steps alone
he oversees his retinue leave home
in slow advance. Between them, silently
the pallid lady moves, smiles, sings,

approaches the dusky monarch courteously,
remarks upon his prowess and his wit,
stands eye to eye, measuring how fit
to make her challenge seriously
now, in gestures he will understand.

The signals given, he moves one pace
aside; whispers into a servant's ear
passing a message to her standing near.
She moves again; reiterates her case
but knows the just and equal outcome must be
    stalemate!

Words and Wool

Was it here we sat,
knitting, with words, and wool,
one lamplit evening –
soft click of consonants
in criss-cross thrust
needling new stitches
from old yarn?

We nattered on, slipped loops,
in a slow unknotting
of some tangled skeins,
plain words unravelling
a twisted understanding;
passing a purl of wisdom
(so we thought), a brightness
on the flat chat of stocking stitch.

Later, we laid the fabrics
side by side – the patterns
matched. The woven jibes
and questions, teasing out of truth,
would form a garment
fit to hug the chilliest heart,
and button up the old disparities.

Ironing

I was ironing when you called,
creased from the wear and tear
and wash of days;
a heap of crumpled thoughts
over your arm, furrows fretting
your usual gaze.

You sat. We shook the garments
into manageable shape,
lay them down,
then let the gentle weight
of quiet attention smooth
the dark frown.

Old linen, and more recent weaves,
we took out, looked at, pressed –
slip, skirt; gist, core.
Tried to give a shape
to tangled thoughts and anguish,
hung them up to air;
no more. Even to share
this homely ritual, served as a pledge
to seal tomorrow's hour.

The Abbey House Gardens, Malmesbury

(In particular, the Knot Garden)

The scent of a thousand roses!
Could it be this
that made me close my eyes,
sensing another world,
something beyond
bright petals and dark gloss of leaf.

Nearby, the knot garden,
saying something more
than its criss-cross
twists of silver, green
and gold, displayed;
its weave of old tried wisdom,

woven to show the hold of knots:
to celebrate
the lacings, links and loops
that bind us each to each,
in loose lasso or tighter hitch,
bowline or bend.

Each knot's laid out in living
greenery; pattern
of all our nettings and entanglements;
the chosen few, and those
that grip us in their mesh
without consent.

Sometimes a skein will tighten,
coiling round a helpless heart,
make us cry
for gentler tendrils, knots
and fastenings to keep us
firm … but free.

This braided foliage
does not slip loose or fall
apart; its knots lie bedded
under August sun and winter showers:
an earthy constancy, upheld
by perfume from a thousand flowers.

Knottings

Remember the reef?
The knot that feels so smoothly intertwined?
Love lying flush,
unaware of pull from either side.
We felt so perfectly symmetric,
matched to a tee, secure,
ready for posting anywhere.

It was not the pulling
either way that would undo us;
rather a gentle pushing in,
towards the centre,
loosening the loops, or,
finding one thread straightening,
the other slipping off.

Maybe a sheetbend
would have shown more foresight,
linking firmly two unequal cords?
A sailor or a Boy Scout
could have told us so.
Yet, the first knot held its own,
survived the fraying, the wear and tear.

I see it change; the twine unwinding,
then rejoining, in a plaited splice,
that should be doubly strong.
It rings a space to be apart in, yet embraced.
A space to hold the almanac
of all our days, dreams and doings.

All the fingered strands
are tightly woven now;
press their pattern into one another,
bear each other's imprint,
strain, question, but cannot unravel.
Hold fast.

Knowing You

You, who I know so well,
   yet do not know,
   marking your glance,
   smile, quiver, gaze,
   criss-cross of fretted brow,
   and long-worn stance
   printed and imprinted
   on my memory's plate.

You, whose wonted
   words and gestures,
   turn of phrase, and
   tune of tongue,
   signal across the space
   between us –

You, walking down
   the long aisles of your eyes
   beyond the communion rail,
   where I cannot follow,
   cannot know where
   the secret chalice lies –

When will the full and holy wine
spill out into the sunlight,
and we, astounded, drink our fill?

Love Song

If you would kiss,
kiss now, and do not calculate.
If you would love,
love now; or maybe fate
will thwart your chance.

If you would learn,
make this hour your beginning.
No one can know
the course of love's bright happening,
set to entrance.

If we would laugh,
laugh now, whilst we are merry.
Step out a pas-de-deux
beneath the flowering cherry.
Come! Quick! Let us dance!

Encounter

I met him in the first week of July.
 He served me such a scorcher
I was too slow to reply.

His next delivery fell right in my court.
 I took a breath, a swing,
then gave a suitable retort.

This brash young fellow's shots came with surprise;
 one fiercely fast, one softer,
one in mysterious guise.

'Love all', was how we started; then went on
 to 'Love fifteen; Love thirty',
but NO loving had begun!

The altercation battled on with zest;
 I wondered what the deuce t'was all about.
Then it rained, and quickly, shelter, rest,

until the sun came out. I served an ace
 and felt six inches taller, till
he smashed my volley to an awkward place.

The argument grew passionate. I thought,
 we might have been the best of friends,
so … why slice my remarks and call it sport?

On and on it went, a long set-to.
　　Not to end evenly, or to compromise.
One had to win; we had to see it through.

Next time I met him, it was in August.
　　We smiled, linked arms and chatted amiably
about the weather, tennis, dieting, and Proust.

Talk of Stars, and Stars

He talks of quasi-stars, black holes,
the less than, less than nothingness,
the stuff of space. Our normal thoughts
collapse, turned inside out.
It goes against our earthly grain
and foothold. Undoes every tether.

A self-devouring universe
gives all grey matter indigestion.
The everlasting flyaway cosmos
leaves a black vacuum where the heart was.
Eyes roll empty along sinking shores.

Remember then one night in hot July.
We slept unroofed, a pinpoint far
from road or dwelling. Faces upturned
towards the lustrous canopy. No earthly
source of light to spoil the jewelled glow.

We lay quite silent, swathed in reverence.
Asked no questions, numbers or measurements.
Only the moment mattered. Even that
dissolved. We lost our names to a thousand
unnamed stars. The dark fields hedged
us round in cool embrace. We slept.

Thoughts on Space and Time

To Make the Headlines

Take a smitten woman, weeping,
by her dying child. Violence
strikes, even from a cloudless sky.
Hover round her hopelessness. Intrude.
Wrench from her whispered anguish
words – to be starred,
strung up, struck home to make
a hard fast scoop.

Take a man, a sport, upright,
caught in the crossfire of hot politics;
losing a foothold, clutching at the web
of truth; falling. Foul him.
Gather round him mike and camera.
Catch a sigh or sound of pleading;
Any words to knock
into a black, sharp shape.

Take a body, take a battle.
Grab a buzzing word
to mock, to fetter in dark print
that will not be forgot.
Hammer home the nails
that fix the morning shock.
Ignore the wounds. Tomorrow's lines
will gloss all ravaged hearts with spick designs –
more startling news to beat the clock.

Another World

They tell me
there's a new world in the offing,
call it 'cyberspace'.

How to get there?
Press the button,
tap the right keys,
watch the screen,
attend!

Your eyes will ride you
to a highway labelled 'super',
crossing deserts of shifting molecules.
Signs lure you on
to faceless countries and encounters.

(You must leave your heart,
and head, behind.)

This is a pitchless void
where no sun shines,
nor light from any eye.
Only a lurid electronic glow
from a dead sky leads you on
to – virtual reality.

Hold my hand! Don't let me go!
I want my head and heart.
I want sun, wind and rain.
I want the close enigma of your eyes again.

Thoughts on Space and Time

I cracked an egg,
sharp, on the basin's rim;
freed the gluten and the gold to fall
and swim within the rounded space.

In the beginning
all we knew of home
was in those warm embracing arms,
a circle of mysterious space.

SO, space is curved
around us; proven by
a thousand calculations and equations;
the endless, captured in the mind.

For us to feel, not prove;
to stand at night, in wonder
at the arching dome of stars
enclosing this familiar home.

As space, so time,
curved round to frame and bound
our days and doings, plantings, reapings,
weepings, and wanderings.

The seasons spiral
into one long rolling coil.
I bend again,
to bed potatoes in dark soil;
observe the rule of space and time.

Gaia's Cloak

She wore a wonderful attire …
long skeins of cloudy voile
clung round her shimmering
azure skirts and golden camisole.
Once, a fine mantle hung around
her shoulders, swayed as she spun;
a textured mix of verdant brilliance
trembled in the sun.

Underneath's a lining near her skin,
and woven in, close stitches hold
a wealth of vibrant jewels.
Pockets too; full of treasures to dispense.
Her great heart beats.
Blood flows in bounty.
Her breath pervades the ether,
celebrating life.

…………………………………

Now her mantle hangs in rags,
not worn, but torn; the seams undone,
her habit vandalised.
Many tug and slash a patch
for profit from those generous folds.
She gives a shiver of distress.
Without her garb, a sickness
spreads its sinister denuding.

No tailor's skill or finger's nimble
flair can mend this cloak.
Its weave is intricate. Long threads
of mystery lie in its glossy nap.
The ancient wisdom calls us to revere
this peerless robe; to hold, to understand;
lest it should wither, and become
fair Gaia's tainted pall.

Astronaut's Reports

(by Edgar Mitchell, Oleg Makarov, and
Vladimir Shatalov)

He said, it was
a sparkling jewel emerging
from behind the moon,
slowly, in great majesty;
a delicate blue sphere
laced with swirling veils
of white; a small pearl
in a thick sea
of dark mystery.

He said, the dawn
is a green-blue line
that fast becomes a rainbow,
hugs the horizon,
then explodes into the sun.

He said, the night is magical;
a darkly silvered sphere
turning in poised solemnity
among a million stars.
Somewhere a storm erupts.
Flashes of fire light up
a continent.

Later, they spoke again,
disturbed by change.
Told how the verdant robe had
shrunk;
the glistening blue had darkened,
that bright sheen dulled,
the lacery begrimed.

This said ... they wept,
fearing the globe condemned,
and all its awesome lustre
lost past reclaim.

"His is the blue music of what is happening"

(From a sonnet by Ciaran Carson about a Zen warrior seeking inner peace)

His are the crystal notes of 'now';
the beat of heart, the beat of feet,
the daily clamour of the street;
the long-drawn sigh, not knowing why
such sorrow stalks the world's sidewalks,
while tears and troubles tear apart
the fragile fabric of the heart.

He is our Zen man, eye on the ball man;
"What is happening" is his concern.
He'll share your story, join your table,
mend your motor, yet is able
to hold each moment to the light,
show you its brightness, till it slips
through his fingers, out of sight.

Blue

Far away is blue and out of mind;
    unreachable,
the lovely dome we often miss because
    we bend to busy-ness.

Our blue ethereal backcloth wraps the world,
    glimpsed between roofs
or leaves, or seen unclouded
    as our buoyant comfort.

Late evenings a sky is azure. There we gaze long,
    almost lose a foothold,
so that death would seem an opening
    into a blue embrace.

Near to, the gentian and the heavenly blue
    entice us inwards, to the hidden
heart. We stare
    into compelling blueness.

Nearer still, these blue veins bind us,
    tooth, nail, heart and head;
spell out our closed mystery –
    the surge of crimson blood.

Tea in the Hospital Ward
by Sir Stanley Spencer

Spread your sandwich soldier.
Lay the ooze of blood-red jam
between white slices.
Cover flayed flesh.
Wrap your shattered heart
between the sombre sheets.

Blot out the stench of fire and flash
with whiffs of disinfectant.
Open your eyes.
This world is passable.
The room is ordered, warm;
there are mugs of tea.

Yes, even comb your hair.
The mud and blood are washed away,
and you might smile,
except that memories
have you by the throat,
will not let you go.

Here is some comfort,
till you feel a cold steel twisting,
"Orders to return to post".
A pen is poised to note your name.
Will it be a dark cross?
Or, maybe, a mark of mercy,
lest you be lost
in grey anonymous dust.

The House That Jack Built

Marmalade

Twelfth night it was, the party season's end.
Next day he came. Something was amiss.
She saw behind his smiling eyes of yesterday
a puckered twist of bitterness.

Her mouth dried, heart hung; she could taste it too –
seeing the basketful of Seville fruit.
"Take these," he said, "do with them what you will.
I've heaved them far enough all on my own."

She weighed them; washed, checked with care each acid
fruit. Then peeled, cut, scraped; searched
to disinter the slippery acrid pips
that, buried there, would add their spike of hatefulness.

The long task done, sweetening was what she sought.
Measures of sugar, fruit, and water mixed,
stirred over the fire's alchemic flame.
She watched the slowly simmering resolution.

Now all is in preserve; glass jars, well labelled.
Nothing is lost, save pips, whose content helped
the whole to gel. A spread to share on morning
toast. A taste of sweetened bitterness.

The Reel Unwinds

We made our debut once. Remember?
My white dress; you in tails, silk tie;
smile upon smile for cameras …
    and each other.

Our parts? … the hero and the heroine,
self-cast, with no director or producer.
We spoke the script, we made the story,
    frame by frame.

Called it a romance, a dream
adventure story bubbling
from day to day, bright with the glint
    of rainbow colours.

Blue sky beginning, then … the going on.
No one to tell us when, or what, or how
the universal story should be told.
    Adam and Eve, again.

Sometimes a clouded lens, a hitch,
a badly twisted tape, the dialogue at odds,
a blackness blotting out the themes we'd chosen.
    Then, we felt lost.

But still the camera ran, from early dawn
until we locked the door, turned out
the lamps, and let the moonlight
        soothe our sorrows.

Still it runs. We say the old familiar lines;
try for fresh renderings, even
a surprise perhaps, a new lilt
        to an old love song.

St Valentine's Day

A day to concentrate the mind,
the heart,
to get the picture back in centre of the frame.

Shall it be close-up, or a distant view?
It should encompass
both the smiling and the pain.

Focus is all. I must adjust the lens
and keep my hands steadfast,
not to distort, or blame

you for a quivering blur.
My camera eye can tip your image over,
skew it. It's a hurtful game.

Sunlight may help to ease discomfort.
Flash that is slick and quick
could falsify the self you claim.

Now is the moment. Press the shutter.
I'll make today's especial print
pinpoint the inscape of your name.

After a Party

There were some links
I might have forged.
A party, on a summer lawn,
under a purple moon,
with candlelight and wine,
warm honeyed scents,
enough to melt the wax
round any isolated cell.

But, as it was with cracks
and laughs, the smiles that strain
to loose the regimented jaw,
I think this morning more
of eyes. I could have ventured in,
tiptoeing the keyhole chink,
towards the private hearth,
where coals might kindle flames
to weld a fragile chain,
before the curtained hour
and bolted door left
but a face and name.

Let Me Now Praise My Four Brown Hens

LET ME NOW PRAISE MY FOUR BROWN HENS

who alight from their perch
as the sun rises, and patiently
await the opening of their door;
who jump eagerly from their house
in due order; share their pan
of meal without dissent.

I observe how they spend their day
in leisurely perambulation,
exploring all corners of their plot.
Each enters the nest-box
as her urge arises, deposits
there a clean, brown egg.

When the day is hot and sunny,
they hollow out a dust bath
in a chosen spot; fluff,
clean and preen their plumage.
When it rains, they shelter
in a small shack without complaint.

If I gather vegetables nearby,
they fly to some high spot
from where they keep watch over me,
gently crooning in companionship.
When they hear me in the garden,
all at the gate, they crowd, in hope.

I bend to stroke them. They submit.
When I change their bedding
for sweet-smelling hay, they
come with curiosity, attend
with interest all procedures,
quietly cluck their acquiescence.

Should they see or sense
a rat, or other mischievous intruder,
straightway they take a stance
of dire alarm; necks stretched
to full; combs high and anxious,
in a dignified forbiddance.

If one should suffer mild
ill-health, she hides away and fasts,
until a soon and full recovery;
then joins her sisters, shares
again the evening corn,
waits for the twilight hour.

Then, one by one, to their
appointed place along the perch;
they join the mystery
of the sleeping world.
Short lives; long days,
to breathe and be, yet not to know.

LET ME NOW PRAISE MY FOUR BROWN HENS.

The House That Jack Built

This was the house that Jack built.
Or – did Jack's house build me?
That four square, fair and solid
framework of my childhood.

"Play the game.
Set goals to aim for.
Do your best in everything.
If at first you don't succeed,
try, try again. Don't cry.
Don't dream. Be a man."

I built my house accordingly.
Or – did my house build me?
It stands here now, right angles
round the space I think I understand.
Precepts were clear.

But then you came, to share
the bounds I thought immutable.
Now, edges fray, straight lines
are frilled. A teasing skein of ribbon
twines from room to room.

I wonder,
was the house that Jack built,
is the one I built myself,
my own?

Monday

Monday's the day when you might see
Mother's blouse out on a spree
Flaunting high its frills and flowers
Oblivious of the threat of showers
Airily an arm she flings
over socks that dance like springs,
and twist and turn about each other,
writhing in the arms of Mother.

Close beside and rather prudish,
Granma's vest swings somewhat sheepish,
Sidling up to Father's shirt …
newly exorcised of dirt.
Is she cajoling? or is she teasing?
Does she find the clean smell pleasing?
"Next to Godliness" she'd say,
but jeans beside her, never pray.
Purposefully frayed and faded,
lean, they walk the world unaided,
striding over Granpa's jacket,
lolling legs beside his pocket.

Granpa gives a woolly smile,
Wryly turns, and with no guile,
watches tights and panties winking,
wondering what the neighbour's thinking.

Bras and stockings, belts and braces
Toss and jaunt in their pegged places,
Straining for a quick release,
and some warm and friendly peace,
leg on leg and arm on chest
folded close and flat to rest
no more chance to run amok
behind the airing cupboard's lock.

Laying Lino, 1951

The day they laid the lino
they were young but it was long –
a twelve foot, rolled up, shiny
cylinder. "We must," he said
"not cut it; joints will
let the water in."

All in one piece, up two steep
flights of narrow stairs
they inched the beast.
The final corner stumped them.
Twelve long feet would not
curve round the bannister.

So, out through the landing window
gingerly, they slid the
macroscopic barber's pole.
A few tense moments, then a swing
and neatly round into a spacious room.
An ancient bath on four claw feet
stood grinning at their sweat.
So, to unroll and fit the gleaming
stuff round toilet furniture,
line up the holes so carefully cut
for those claw feet, a task requiring
engineering skill. The only way –
unroll, and lay the burden
on one partner's back!

Thus could the hump be slowly,
slowly, levelled into place,
an operation long and tedious;
with anxious, muffled comments
and instructions reaching someone
underneath, whose quietly
flattening body wondered
if she ever would get out!

She did! At last the dingy room
sprang into brilliant chequered life;
winked at their efforts, and
as far as I recall, they kissed.

Lost Poems

Poems We Have Known

Most poems spend their days pressed flat,
hardly ever see the light of day.
Some lie low on backs of envelopes;
letters answered, poems not quite complete.

Some have been lucky. A chosen few
travel by tube. Paddington to Kew.
Others take flight on the breath of song,
ring out from Wigmore Hall, school choir, or singalong.

This one will live a day; to celebrate
a change. Today the earth will start
to turn its northern climes towards the sun;
light will begin to creep up on the morning tea and toast.
New poems may stir, take shape, may find their feet.

Lost Poems

Lately I've been losing poems.
They've been slipping through my fingers,
dodging the darts I throw to try and pin them.

I saw one sidling among
the shadows on a sunlit lawn;
another hid behind an awesome door

I could not open. I left one once
between the pages of a newspaper,
close to the picture of an anguished mother

clutching treasured photos. Sometimes
I catch a glimpse … roll out a poem
on the pastry board; see a corner

showing in some stranger's pocket;
notice lines across a thoughtful brow,
a glint in a lively eye, a reflection

in a mirror, or a tear. I hear
a whispering under the trees at dusk,
Orlando's verses faintly fluttering … telling

how the heart beats, how we feel
the world's pulse surge around us:
a million teasing mysteries all here and now,

waiting to be netted, worded, shaped.
Lost poems to retrieve.
Moments to arrest. New poems to weave.

Supper After Reading *End Game* by Samuel Beckett

Pass the pepper spouse.
This dish is flavourless.
Is there no one in the house
who knows when all this tediousness

is going to end? What's that?
The gate? So, is he coming yet?
Are those his footsteps on the parapet?
Keep quiet. Keep calm. I think I smell a rat.

He always said he'd come
and tell us what to do. The salt –
it needs salt too. It's underdone.
You always say that. Bolt

the door. We don't want a disturbance.
He might upset our appetite
or ask where we are going. Glance
through the window. Is the light

fading yet? Is it the beginning?
The beginning of the end?
You make me sick. Grinning
like a Cheshire cat. I'd send

for the doctor. But he wouldn't know
if it was time yet, or what to do.
Have you finished supper? No?
Will we finish before he comes,
before the final whistle blows?

Plans for the Poet's Festival

I shall wear
my multi-coloured tee shirt,
logo of the poet's club,
in fluorescent blaze across
my back (ten biros rampant
on a mountain of discarded verse).

I shall juggle
with a hundred metaphors,
sending them chasing one another
in a crazy arc, tumbling;
and spinning round my head; until
the verbal vertigo sets in.

We shall dance,
trailing scarves of synonyms, skipping,
and tapping out the syllables;
twisting the trochaic metre, twirling
words into a dizzy pirouette,
that ends on one full-stop.

And we shall drink,
bottles of Muse's booze, the good
old cordial, topped up with tips
from those who've won acclaim;
the clever rhymers, moderns, or old timers,
the witty, the worthy, all celebrating word-bibbers.

Private View

A white line and two posts,
frame for the weekly ritual.

She pegs pyjamas high, then,
looking higher still, spellbound,
sees gold robinia, luminous,
against the bluest sky of summer;
heraldic brilliance, defying every
gleaming pigment on the palette.

This is the private view.
No tickets, wine or jostling.

Only the gentle flap of sheets,
shimmer of breeze on leaves;
no one else to share the moment's glory.
She makes a mirror print,
beds it deep;
a keepsake for her hidden gallery.

The Wedding of Elaine and Patrick

August 2005

Take your partner for the wedding dance,
the day by day, the come what may,
the all the way dance.

Maybe you'll swing, among these flowers;
twirl a reel, with family and friends;
slow waltz beneath the stars.

You may dance the day long; breakfast,
lunch and supper, tango or rhumba,
side by side, or face each other.

Rock, roll, polka, through wind and rain.
When storms blow up, change step and find
the way back home again.

Today you're here to share with us
your love for one another, as we offer –
each – our benediction.

This is your hey-day; pas-de-deux day,
centre stage, to celebrate
the bond of constancy.

Even when the feet are weary
you'll still dance on – because
the heart knows how
to keep the beat. It knows the steps,
and it can lead, day in,
day out, and all the way.

Scene from School Sports Day

Take your partners
for the three-legged race!
Choose carefully
for this requires more
than a pretty face.

Do you take this boy to be …
this girl? to share a leg?
No rings or vows,
but you'll be bound. A scarf
will do to tie two legs together.

Then arm in arm,
or maybe arms round waists.
You're ready!
Remember now, no haste,
but find your pace
and move together in a rhythmic step:
learn about each other.

You've practised? All the better!
Any rush towards success
will surely bring a fall:
and then, to get upright again's
the hardest part of all.

Ready: steady: off you go!
Counting may help
or some well-known refrain:
but once you think and act as one.
You're nearly home.

Keep going! Don't be drawn
to look at others.
Watch your step and look ahead.
You lost your grip and wobbled once,
but all was well. You're there!
Over the touchline (not the first)
one hot and happy pair.

So, what comes next?
Let's get untied.
Is it the egg and spoon?
The gentle cradling
of a fragile thing,
demanding different skills,
– a softer tune?

The Last Waltz

This is the time for the slow waltz,
the last waltz, nearing the party's end.
We've done the quickstep, foxtrot, tango;
held each other close to twirl
the faster waltzes of the past;
relished the final dizzying spin.

The pace is slower now. We step
through flickering shadows, dimming lights,
out into the grey and silver night,
under the stars and tall mysterious trees.
No one knows when we must part.
But still the dance goes on
in hidden chambers of the heart.

Loaf or Lyric?

Sometimes an aroma teases,
sends a shiver to your roots.
Sometimes a flash, or flit of wing,
a thing to latch on,
hold in hollow of the palm,
wondering such crumbly leaven
could be germ, gist, hint
of a given shape, to prove, in time.

So, to foster this elusive yeast,
inert, until we warm and sweeten it.
Attending then, with measured steps
we mix, mould, stretch: pull
and roll the dough with diligence,
shaping to loaves, lyrics, lines,
that bear the ferment of the first insight.

Then – waiting – until,
hot from the heart or pen,
we see a shape to recognise,
familiar; ancestral form,
yet new-born. A novelty,
to taste; perhaps to share.

End of Season Apple

Gale Force

No one seems to be in charge tonight.
There's a madness in the air.
Trees swing in a frenzied turmoil,
branches lash the sky and roar.

A loud titanic force has swept
away their calm and dignity. Everything
I thought familiar seems unhinged
and on the rampage, raging headlong

on and on relentlessly; a dark
forceful intensity ...
running amok ... making its mark;

telling us in no uncertain terms
our place within the cosmic scheme;
turning us inside out, so that
we lose hold of our comfortable dream.

I pull my collar up; don't want to know;
bend to the onslaught, head down,
tottering steps towards some haven
to await reprieve, and the ending of the storm.

Weather Forecast

Today the charts show cloud
   across the British Isles.
      There will be
mist and murk on the moors,
drizzle dallying in the dales.
Gales will gust and gallivant
     and keep us guessing.
(You will need your scarf.)
Hail may harass the heaths and hills;
snow sweep the slopes then settle;
frost lead to frightful icy patches.
(Advice is – stay at home.)

Further weather warnings follow:
lightning may strike you anywhere;
a thunder bolt; freak floods;
a troublesome tornado at tea time.
      The sky may fall!
Umbrellas will be no protection.
So, do take care, and if confused
ring "weather-wise 074"
for an improved selection.

Tomorrow will be clear and sunny –
   for the time of year.

Kingfisher

Two sightings in sixty years is all I claim.
Yet, every day, this emerald scimitar cuts
shimmering air somewhere, pinpoints his prey.

I saw him skim a river in a French valley;
a streak of turquoise, mirroring highlights
in the dark pool of a lover's gaze.

Years later, end of a burnishing day,
when children's limbs were tired from day long
dipping, dredging and splashing in a bright pool,

I saw him up the shadowed tunnel
of the stream; an azure statue, sentinel,
upon a watching post, until, something unseen

released an instant spring, a flash, a needling dive.
A trice … he's back, as though he'd never left,
except for dripping silver loot held forceps firm.

The young made their own moments,
pearls on a skein of weeds. They missed
the meteoric dart of wings I saw …

my brightly jewelled memento, pinned
on the dappled cloak that wrapped
the darkly flowing water's tresses.

Leaves Falling and Turning

Let the leaves fall.
Do not grieve.
Their day is done.
A pall of rose-gold covers all
the too ripe rotting fruitfulness.

Let the leaves turn.
Do not fret.
Words that are writ
will age and fade, become as dust
on musty shelves, unread, or tended.

Let the leaves fall.
Gather but one.
Marvel the sum
of all that veined and lithesome beauty
that hung and trembled in the sun.

Let the leaves turn,
But mark the one
where words have set alight a flame
for you, let them become your own.

Knowing Some Apples

Some things must be taken here and now,
the moment fixed. Red Medlars shining on the bough
above your head. Reach up and take one!
Pierce the crimson skin. The juice will spurt
and dribble down your chin; teeth part
and crunch flesh pinkened by the August sun.
   Know it now.

Another fruit demands more patient care.
Pick in October when the day is fair;
lifting the apple gently, break
it from the tree. Lie it soft in a basket,
to be set apart in a cool and airy spot,
secure from rodents, or the frost's attack.
The Russets' and the Sturmers' flesh will mellow
slowly, while the Earth lies cold and fallow.
   Know it then.

Come back to August. On a nearby tree
of apples, see pellucid lanterns curiously
lit by the slanting sun. Examine
these, and find all flesh within the skin
removed, leaving a perfect sphere, a gold
and waxy shell … the White Transparent's bold
deceit. The wasps were there before us; left
these baubles, tricks, to round our knowing,
   and their theft.

Weeds

We have planted
a garden between us,
beds, borders, and orchard,
reaching trees and
weeping shrubs;
but still, there are
bitter weeds that rankle.

I tasted one today.
You made a potion
from the pods, and
held it to my tongue.
Quassia-like
it burned my throat
steeped and sickened,
strangled my gut.

I could not spit
or spew; only swallow,
ingest, and know
I must have sown
these acrid seeds
among the garden flowers.

End of Season Apple

The garden has an end of season feel.
Seedheads replace bright flowers we grew.
Piled autumn litter covers all
the tended beds. The paths criss-crossed
with muddied prints of boot and shoe;
the thousand times we passed.

I see you bend to lift
an apple hidden in the tufted grass;
examine, taste, discard its rotting core.
You pick a rosier one; rub it on your sleeve,
bring back the tempting sheen it bore.

I cross the space between us,
saying, "Take a bite!
Is it as sweet as ever,
lying there so long?"
The juice runs down your chin.
I take a share,
tasting a hint of wine
to celebrate our fitful season.

"Come! Apple of my eye!
The light is fading,
but the hearth's still bright.
Let us go in."

Acknowledgements

I give particular thanks to Cathy O'Neill who has been such a constant source of support and given her time so generously over the last two years. To Sara Thielker for such lovely illustrations, which so carefully depict the delicacy of the natural world. To Hilary Sawyer for so carefully typing up all the poems, many from hand-written scripts. And of course to my mother for leaving such a rich legacy for her children, grandchildren, wider family and friends to enjoy.

Elaine McCurdy